Snooker Rules OK

Geoff Hales

Illustrations by Bryan Flaherty

A & C Black · London

*To Mike, Les and John, for the balls we couldn't
sink and the comments I couldn't use*

First published 1987 by
A & C Black (Publishers) Limited
35 Bedford Row, London WC1R 4JH

ISBN 0 7136 5624 7

Hales, Geoff
   Snooker rules OK.
   1. Snooker
   I. Title
   794.7'35   GV900.S6

   ISBN 0-7136-5624-7

Printed and bound in Great Britain by
A. Wheaton & Co. Ltd, Exeter

Contents

Introduction

Snooker is such a civilised game. A large crowd sits in
respectful silence and listens to the click of balls as they
glide over the green cloth. There is a polite round of
applause, and a call of 'One hundred and nineteen'. 'The
young man from Tooting's perfectly on the blue' breathes
the commentator reverently, 'and there's not a thing the old
Welsh wizard can do about it'. The cameras swing to the old
Welsh wizard, who grins toothily. Everybody knows the
rules, and no one ever gets upset — well, almost no one. And
there is a referee. All the players have to worry about is
left-hand side, that extra money for the highest break of the
tournament and which waistcoat to wear in the Vladivostok
Masters on Thursday. As I said, it's such a civilised game!

There exists, however, a less exalted level of snooker,
where there are no teams of experts in the commentary box,
no referee, and not much danger of racing to one hundred
and nineteen and finding yourself perfectly on the blue. At
the humbler end of the game, a player whose short-term
ambition is to win a pint of keg and a bag of prawn cocktail
crisps, and who dreams of one day making a break of

twenty, may struggle to seven and find himself snookered on all the colours. He spends five minutes chalking his cue, looks at the problem from six different angles, has a go off two cushions at the distant brown, misses it, hits the blue, cannons on to the pink and goes in-off. He retreats cursing and mutters something about 'four away' because he was going for the brown, but his opponent, a hard man, says it must be six because he went in off the pink and that's higher. They discuss it. Disturbed by the controversy, the chaps at the next table chip in and and suggest it might be five. No one is quite sure, but after a while this is accepted as a happy compromise. In fact, five is right, because blue was the first ball struck.

Little problems of this sort arise all the time when players already occupied with tactical considerations have to be their own referees as well. What happens, for instance, if you play away from a touching ball which is 'on' and you hit another ball which is not? Is that a foul? And suppose you pot it? Is that one? If so, how many do you give away? Not sure? Well, what you need is a copy of this book . . .

The Rules

Every player, whether a professional, a serious club player or a once-a-week bungler who watches too much television, should be familiar with the rules of snooker. This book, though delightfully entertaining and highly instructive, is not intended as a substitute for the official version, which is available from the governing body of the game, The Billiards and Snooker Control Council, Coronet House, Queen Street, Leeds, West Yorkshire LS1 2TN. Local clubs and snooker centres should have copies for sale, too, and the rules are often displayed in a glass case overlooking the tables where everyone can see them but hardly anyone bothers to look at them.

When you do read the rules, don't be put off by what appears to be yards and yards of regulations hanging on the wall. They are very clearly written, and you should be able to find your way round them without much trouble. The days are gone when you discovered reds referred to as 'pyramid balls' ('pyramids' was a fore-runner of snooker), in-offs (when the cue-ball enters a pocket after striking another ball) called 'losing hazards' and the game itself solemnly sub-titled 'Snooker's Pool'. A 'snooker', by the way, was a contemptuous term for a first-year cadet at Woolwich Military Academy.

Most players learn the rules by hearsay. They play for the first time and pick up the rules as they go along. When something happens, they ask 'What do I do now?' Their opponents tell them what they were told when they started playing. This information may or may not be accurate, and can lead to all sorts of misunderstandings when they come across someone who was told something else 'by a bloke who's been playing for years'.

Snooker Rules OK is designed to help both the beginner and the bloke who's been playing for years.

Setting Up

The rules tell us that the game is played 'on an English
Billiard Table'. This is of some importance, because
continental tables have no pockets, while old-style Chinese
tables, though they do have the full quota of six pockets, are
circular.

A full-sized snooker table is 12ft long and 6ft wide. With
cushion overhang the actual playing area is 11ft 8½in. by 5ft
10in. It is about 2ft 10in. high and weighs about 1¾ tons,
most of which is the slates from which the bed is made.
There is also what the rules call 'the standard table —
metric', whose dimensions are actually in millimetres. For
those interested in such curiosities, the playing area of a
metric table measures 3,500mm×1,750mm, with a
tolerance of plus or minus 3mm.

The official distance across the pocket openings is supposed to 'conform to the templates authorised by the Billiards and Snooker Control Council', but there are tables with pockets where it does not. We have all played on tables where the pockets actually seem smaller than the balls, but that may be a delusion suffered on one of those days when we feel we couldn't hit the Crucible Theatre with a water melon. The size of the pockets is, in fact, quite important (at least to some of us), because, to gain official recognition, breaks of 147 have to be made on tables whose pocket openings are of the correct width or 'cut'.

The end of the table where the black is placed is known as the top cushion, and the other end, quite naturally, is called the bottom cushion. This is also called the baulk end, and the line drawn across the table, 29in. from the bottom cushion and parallel to it, is the baulk line. The 'D', in the centre of this line, has a radius of 11½in. 'Baulk' is a billiards term that has no other application to the rules of snooker. There are no restrictions about playing behind it from the 'D' as there are in billiards. 'Up the table' means playing towards the top cushion and 'down the table' towards the baulk end.

Most people will realise there are fifteen reds, except on the standard six-feet table where there are only ten. They are each $2\frac{1}{16}$in. in diameter (as are all the balls), and they are arranged in the shape of a triangle behind the pink. The apex of the triangle should be as near as possible to the pink without actually touching it. The black occupies the spot nearest the top cushion. The pink is placed on what is still known as the pyramid spot, the next one to the black as you look down the table towards the 'D'. The blue goes on the centre spot. The green, brown and yellow balls are placed on the three spots on the baulk line, the green on the left, the brown in the middle and the yellow on the right as you look up the table. 'G.B.Y.' or 'God Bless You', is the conventional way of remembering the order. I have tried, but I cannot think of anything more exciting. The cue-ball can be placed anywhere in the 'D' for the break shot (or when playing from the 'D' at any time), as long as it does not touch the green, brown or yellow.

One more word about placing. Pints should not be placed on the edge of the table where they can be knocked over by cue-ends. This is a dangerous, wasteful and potentially expensive practice, beer being the price it is. Cues, by the way, must not be less than 3ft long — most are about 4ft 10in. — and, the rules warn, 'shall show no substantial departure from the traditional and generally accepted shape and form'. So, if you were thinking of fitting telescopic sights, don't.

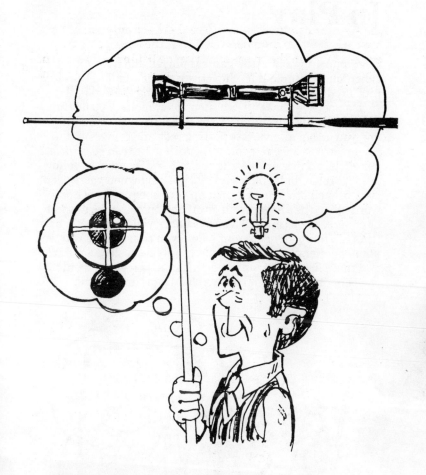

The rules permit the use of rests, but it is worth mentioning at this point that it is up to the players to put them on the table, to put them back after the stroke, and to bear the attendant responsibility for seeing that they don't foul any ball.

Finally, any very keen player will be able to tell you that the reds score one point each, the yellow two, the green three, the brown four, the blue five, the pink six and the black seven. No problems so far. The difficulties start when you come to the table. This is when you have to hit the wretched things.

In Play

Everyone knows how the game is played and how ridiculously simple it is. You strike the cue-ball so that it hits a red. The red enters a pocket, leaving the cue-ball in such a position that you can then pot a colour. You do that. The cue-ball is now lying where you can pot another red, and you go on, alternately potting reds and colours — the colours are at once re-spotted — until all fifteen reds have gone. Then you start potting the colours, in order — yellow, green, brown, blue, pink and black — and when you've done that, all you have to do is pick up your cheque, have a few words with the viewers and go off and open a supermarket or endorse something. If by any chance you fail to pot a ball (this can happen) or commit a foul, you retire gracefully and your opponent has a go. It could hardly be easier, could it? But there are a few points worth having a look at, if only for the benefit of those who miss a shot from time to time.

The break shot

The players decide the order of play by whatever method
suits them, and must then stick to that order throughout the
frame. The winner of the toss does not necessarily break, but
most players find it an advantage to do so. The break shot is
played from hand (from the 'D'), and the player breaking
must aim to hit the reds, either directly or off as many
cushions as he likes. (The cue-ball is 'in hand' after entering
a pocket or coming to rest off the table.)

   Many people seem to think that if the striker mis-hits the
cue-ball or misses the pack, he can simply have another try,
because it's 'only the break shot'. This is not so. Once the tip
of the cue has touched the cue-ball, a stroke has been played,
the game has begun and there are no second tries.

There is another myth that on the break shot the striker is allowed to roll the cue-ball up to a cushion and leave it there, giving his opponent awkward cueing and getting himself disliked, but this is quite wrong, too. Deliberate misses are not permitted at any time. If the player who has the first shot fails to make contact with the reds, he gives four away, or more if he hits blue, pink or black instead, and his opponent plays the cue-ball from where it comes to rest. It is not returned to the 'D' unless it goes into a pocket, or if it comes to rest in the angle of a pocket as the result of a foul and cannot then be played directly on to the ball 'on', in this case, one of the reds. If it is 'angled' in this way, the next player can play it from the 'D' or ask the player who angled it to play it himself. This applies at all times when the cue-ball is angled after a foul.

If the second player is snookered as the result of a foul break shot, or indeed after any foul, he may ask his opponent to play the cue-ball again from where it lies, or he may claim a free ball. Free balls are explained later, on page 26. You cannot, by the way, claim a free ball simply because you are unable to get at any particular red on the table. As long as you can 'see' one, you are not snookered and you are required to play at it or to ask your opponent to play if you don't like the position.

Two at a time

You are not allowed to strike two balls simultaneously with the cue-ball, unless they are two reds, or a nominated (free) ball and the ball 'on'. (A ball 'on' is any ball that can legally be hit with the first contact of the cue-ball. When reds are on the table, and the striker is playing for reds, as many as fifteen balls may be 'on' at once. So, if you pot a red, any one of the colours is then 'on', but once you have nominated one that is the only ball 'on'. If you pot it, the reds are then 'on' again.) This means that if you are snookered on a red — the ball 'on' — as the result of a foul, and you have chosen the green as your free ball, you are permitted to hit the green and a red at the same time.

You can pot two or more reds from the same shot and, if you do, you score one for each red. You do not, however, get two chances at the colours. You are not permitted to pot a red and a colour or two colours at once, unless they are the nominated ball and the ball 'on'. If this happens, the ball 'on' is scored. If, by chance, you play at the free ball and knock in the ball 'on', that is quite legal and again the ball 'on' is scored. Free balls are always placed on the table again when potted.

Ball on the edge

There is the possibility that a ball left on the very edge of a pocket by the previous shot may fall in when the next shot is made, without being touched. In such a case neither player gets any points and the ball is simply replaced. This applies even to reds, which normally stay down however sunk.

However, if it happens that the ball which falls from the lip into the pocket would have been hit 'by any ball involved in a stroke', all the balls are replaced and the shot is taken again. So, if a red that you were going to sink at the end of a stylish plant disappears as the result of vibration before it can be struck, you can have another go at it.

A ball that hesitates for a moment on the lip of the pocket and then drops in is not brought back to the lip, even if it looks as if it has stopped.

Re-spotting

Colours potted following the sinking of a red, or as free balls, or as the result of a foul, are at once re-spotted. (One exception to this is the case of the final black — see page 64 for details.) Reds, however, are never put back on the table, except ones that fall in without the striker being responsible. Even reds that go down in the course of a foul stroke stay down, although the foul might benefit the player who committed it by removing a red his opponent might need to pot. There is no spot on which to put a red back.

You may be surprised to know that the striker, not the referee, is responsible for seeing that the balls are correctly replaced when necessary, although we always see the referee doing this on television. Moreover, it is a foul to play a stroke or continue a break with the balls wrongly spotted or not spotted at all. If you do play on in this situation, you count all the points scored up to the moment your opponent

scratches his head and says 'Here, wait a minute, the yellow's on the green spot!' The break ends, the penalty is exacted, and your opponent comes to the table.

There is another bizarre possibility. Imagine that your opponent pots a colour and either fails to re-spot it or re-spots it wrongly, and neither of you notices. He plays on, and in due course it is your turn. After you have played a couple of shots, one of you sees that something is not quite right. What do you do? Who loses points? The answer to this is that all your opponent's points stand because you condoned his foul by not claiming it at the time. You keep any points you have scored up to the moment the mistake is detected, but you give away the appropriate penalty points because it is a foul to play with the balls wrongly spotted. The rules are quite clear that it is the striker's responsibility to see that everything is in order before playing. As you are now the striker, you are responsible. The break ends, and the colour comes up if it was in a pocket, but it remains where it lies if it is on the table.

Re-spotting balls is no problem even to the most modest intellect, but problems may arise when a home spot is occupied by another ball. Here the rule is that the ball to be re-spotted is put back on the spot of the highest value ball which is unoccupied, not on the spot nearest to its own. So, if the green, for instance, is potted and cannot go back on its own spot, it is put on the black spot if that is available. If it is not, it goes on the pink spot, and so on in descending order to the yellow spot. Incidentally, for a spot to be unoccupied, you should be able to place a ball on it without the ball touching any other ball.

But what do you do if all the spots are occupied? The situation becomes a little complicated here. A 'minor' colour — yellow, green, brown and blue — must go as near as possible to its own spot on a line between the spot and the nearest part of the top cushion, without touching another ball. The pink and black, if homeless, are to be placed as near as possible to their own spots, up the table, and in a straight line to the nearest part of the top cushion, just as in the case of the minor colours. However, if there is no space, they have to go as near as possible to their spots down the table, again in a straight line, and of course without touching anything else.

There's just one more thing. If two colours are to be re-spotted and there are problems about where to put them, the highest value ball is spotted first.

Touching ball

If the cue-ball comes to rest touching another ball, you are not allowed to play that ball, even if it is the ball 'on', because that would be a push-shot, which is illegal. You have to play away from it, and without disturbing it in any way. The ball 'on', you will remember, is a ball that can be legally hit with the first contact of the cue-ball.

If you are playing away from the ball 'on', you are considered to have played a fair shot already, simply by starting the stroke with the cue-ball touching a ball which could legally be struck. You are therefore allowed to hit any other ball, whether it is 'on' or not, without penalty. So, if you are 'on' reds and actually touching one, you can play away from it and hit any other ball, even the black, or no ball at all. You can also pot any ball 'on' in playing away from a touching ball which is 'on', but if you pot a ball which is not 'on', that is a foul. For example, if you are 'on' reds and are touching one, you can pot another red, but not a colour.

You can hit a ball which is not 'on', but you must not pot it. It is also a foul if you pocket the cue-ball, directly or off another ball.

If you are touching a ball that is not 'on', you have to play away from it and try to hit one which is 'on'. So, if you are on reds but are touching the blue, you must try to hit a red, however awkward it is. It is not enough just to play away from the blue, and of course you must not touch the blue in playing the shot. If you do, you are considered to have struck it, and, as it is not 'on', that is a foul. You could also be penalised for missing the ball 'on' (in this case, a red) or for hitting any other ball, or for pocketing the cue-ball itself, directly or indirectly. A situation fraught with peril, in fact, and teeming with penalties.

It is one of the referee's jobs, if you are lucky enough to have one of these demi-gods to watch over you, to tell you if the balls are touching. He will do this without being asked.

If the cue-ball appears to be touching more than one ball, he will go further and tell you which it is touching — if you ask him nicely. That is as far as he will go, however. The rules state firmly that he will give no other information, not even for ready money.

Angled

As I said earlier, you are 'angled' if the cue-ball is trapped in the jaws of a pocket in such a way that it is impossible for you to play in a straight line (that is, without using swerve or coming off a cushion) to any part of every ball 'on'. If this happens to you in the course of your own break, you have to get out of it yourself just as you would if you snookered yourself. If your opponent angles you in the course of a fair stroke, that, too, is your bad luck. However, if you are angled as the result of a foul, the referee will state 'angled ball' and then you can either move the cue-ball to the 'D' and play from hand, or ask your opponent to play it from where he left it. Real show-offs with big leads can choose to play it from the angle themselves, but must attempt to hit a ball 'on'. You do not get a free ball. It is quite likely in that situation that you would not be able to see one anyway.

Snookered

The rules say that to be snookered means that 'a direct stroke in a straight line to any part of every ball "on" ' cannot be played because a ball or balls not "on" are in the way. You have to be able to hit either side of the ball 'on' without hitting another ball simultaneously, which means in effect that there has to be the diameter of a ball on either side of the object ball. If you cannot do this after your opponent fouls, you can have a free ball. If you are playing from the 'D', you are snookered on the ball 'on' only if you cannot hit it from anywhere in the 'D' or from any point on the lines. If you are snookered by more than one ball, the nearest to the cue-ball is regarded as the snookering ball.

Snookering is an alternative to potting and is a perfectly legitimate tactic. You can leave your opponent snookered at any time. You can also leave him in a snooker in escaping from the one he set for you — if you're good enough, that is.

And it is not quite unknown for even the best players to leave themselves snookered. In any of those situations, the player simply has to get himself out as best he can and take the consequences if he fails. So, if you do leave yourself stuck behind the pink and black and unable to get at any of the fourteen remaining reds, the only possible consolation may be 'Pint if I get out of this one?'

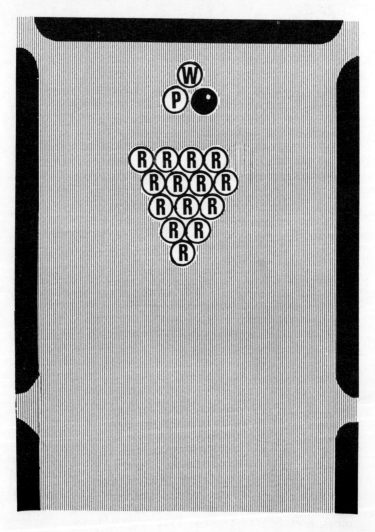

Free ball

If your opponent fouls and leaves you snookered, as defined in the last section, you are entitled to a free ball. The referee, if he is satisfied that you really cannot get at any ball 'on', will award this.

Having a free ball means that instead of the ball 'on' which you now cannot hit fully, if at all, you can nominate any other ball and play at that instead. In nominating you declare which ball you propose to hit first. So, if you are 'on' reds but are snookered behind the black because of your opponent's foul shot, you can nominate the black and play it as if it was a red. If you miss it, that is of course a foul. If you pot the nominated ball, it counts the value of the ball 'on'. It is re-spotted at once, and then you can play for any colour in the usual way, including the black you just potted as a red (it now counts seven again). Then you take another red, and so on.

Occasionally you may play at a nominated ball and pot the ball 'on' with the same shot. For example, if you nominate the black because you can't hit a red, then hit the black and pot a red with the same stroke, it counts one and you carry on. If you pot red and black, you score two (not eight). It is as if you had potted two reds. You are, as mentioned earlier, allowed to strike the ball 'on' and the nominated ball simultaneously.

There is one restriction when you have a free ball. You are not allowed to snooker your opponent behind the nominated ball. You cannot just run up behind the black you nominated and leave your opponent behind it, though you can snooker him behind another ball. You can snooker behind the free ball only if the pink and black are the only balls still on the table.

If you get a free ball when all the reds have been potted, the same rules apply. If you are snookered on the yellow after a foul by your opponent, you can nominate any other ball to serve as the yellow — the brown, perhaps. You pot the brown and score two, the value of the yellow. The brown is re-spotted, and then you play the yellow. If you pot the brown and the yellow with the same shot, you score two just the same, but in this case the yellow stays down, the brown comes up, and you move on to the green. The free ball is always put back on its spot, even if it happens to be the next ball 'on'.

You don't have to say which ball you are nominating, by the way, unless the referee asks you. But it's a good idea to say which one you're going for, especially in self-refereed games, which tend to be the ones in which intention is not always the same thing as result.

The impossible shot

There are some shots which are simply impossible to play without fouling. Imagine, for instance, that you have the cue-ball on the very lip of the pocket, perhaps in the angle as well, and it is right behind the black when you are 'on' something else. There is no room to squeeze past the black on either side, and no amount of swerve will do you any good. Whatever you do, you are sure to hit the black and concede seven. Of course, if you were left in that position by your opponent's foul, you could ask him to play again and look forward to picking up the seven points yourself, or you could claim a free ball if you thought that was to your advantage. But in this case the stroke that left you in a mess was legal and you have to play a stroke. Even the jump shot has been made illegal. So what do you do?

Well, the rules are quite clear on this. Even if the ball 'on' is completely impossible, the striker must try to hit it, and whatever he does will be considered an attempt to do so. Deliberate misses are not allowed. You have to play the shot as well as you can, knowing very well that it is going to mean seven down the wastepipe. What is more, you cannot leave another snooker, deliberately or otherwise, because you will only be asked to play again or concede a free ball. Playing again will probably cost you another seven, making fourteen in all. The young men from Tooting and the old Welsh wizards of this world can laugh off the odd fourteen, but it takes some of us eleven reds and a green to get that many. You just have to bite the bullet, play the shot and hope you don't do too much damage.

The miss

A 'miss', which you sometimes hear called during televised games, is a deliberate miss that happens when the striker is snookered (or very awkwardly placed) and he calculates that to get out of the situation will leave him in so much trouble that it is better for him to forfeit the points for missing the ball 'on' than to make a real attempt to hit it. Hitting it may mean that his opponent is left with an easy shot on a vital ball with perhaps a decisive break to follow, so, compared with that, seven away is inconsiderable, especially to a player with a big lead who could still lose it if his opponent 'gets in'. However, playing to miss is clearly unfair to an opponent who may have played a very skilful stroke to get that snooker and deserves to receive the full benefit of his skill. Of course, he may have been just lucky, but even so he has to be allowed to enjoy his luck and not be cheated out of it.

The rule, therefore, is just as in the 'impossible' shot: the striker must 'to the best of his ability endeavour to hit the ball "on" '. If the referee decides that the striker has not made a genuine attempt, he awards a foul and exacts the penalty. He then offers the player who set up the position the option of having the balls replaced so that the offender has to have another shot at it. The non-striker can, if he wishes, play the stroke himself from where the cue-ball stops. The balls can be set up repeatedly as long as the referee is convinced that the striker is not trying. If he does try, and fouls, the non-striker has the usual option of asking him to play again if he does not like the position, or of having a free ball if he is snookered. If, by any chance, the striker scores on being asked to replay, the points count. This is hardly likely, of course, since he would hardly be playing to miss if there was a chance of scoring by playing a fair shot, but it could happen.

Whether a player is deliberately 'missing' or not is very difficult to judge. The referee has to assess not only what the ball did, but what he thinks the striker meant it to do. You can reasonably suppose that a professional could hit or get pretty close to anything he wanted to as long as it was not absolutely impossible, but it would still be a difficult decision. With lesser players, such as you and me, especially me, it is almost impossible, since we so often fail by wide margins to bring off shots we were genuinely trying for. In these circumstances I suppose we assume that we are trying all the time. You really need a referee for this one.

The deliberate miss used to be one of the aspects of 'wilfully or persistently unfair' play for which the referee could disqualify a player. A second deliberate miss would have been enough for snooker's equivalent of the red card. Now, however, on the rare occasions when a 'miss' is called, the requirement to play again seems to have the desired effect.

Fast play

Snooker is an exciting game — though I have known people who don't think so — and to watch Whirlwind This, Hurricane That and Tornado The Other racing round the table in a blur of fancy waistcoat and piling up century breaks in the time it takes to eat a custard cream is truly mind-blowing. You don't have to break the world land speed record, though.

It is a foul if you are in such a hurry to get on with the break that you play your next stroke before all the balls have stopped moving from the last one. It is also a foul to play before they have come to rest from a shot of your opponent's, however keen you are to get at what he's left you. So wait till they've stopped. See 'Fouls' and 'Penalties' for what happens to you if you can't.

Slow play

On the other hand, you might find yourself playing the kind of opponent who thinks that Eddie Charlton is a hasty young whippersnapper who ought to take a bit more time over his shots. This kind of player shuffles from his chair as if he's getting out of bed on a bad morning, strolls five times round the table for exercise, scratches himself for a while,

chalks his cue, blows all the chalk off, chalks it again, wipes
it with a damp cloth, waves it vaguely over the table and
holds it there like a fisherman waiting for a big one to come
along, takes his chewing gum out, looks for somewhere to
stick it, squats, squints, looks at a few angles, lines up a
shot, addresses the ball several times, changes his mind,
lines up another, goes back to the first, settles over it, gets
up and walks away because his concentration's been
disturbed by a sudden movement three tables away, comes
back, picks up a piece of fluff, has the cue-ball cleaned,
checks the scoreboard, reaches for the half-butt and puts it
back again, blows his nose and says, 'Bit tricky this one,
don't want to rush it, do we?' By the time you've been to the
lavatory, and rung home to say you'll be late for dinner and
you'll get a take-away on the way home and there's no need
to be like that about it, he's played the shot, potted it, and is
going into his routine again. This can be irritating,
especially if you're paying for the table.

There is no time limit for playing a shot, and you don't
have to play quickly just because your opponent likes it that
way. Some players are naturally slower than others. But if
the referee thinks you are playing slowly simply to irritate
your opponent, he can warn the offender that he runs the
risk of being disqualified if he continues to take 'an
abnormal amount of time' over playing his strokes. Again,

that is fine if you have a referee. The rules always assume that you have. If you haven't, you have to sort it out for yourselves. Personally, I always bring a good book. You could even bring this one.

Ball forced off the table

There is never any doubt, of course, that the ball is off the table when you hit it so hard that it lands on the floor, runs off into the car park and comes to rest under a pro's Bentley. That's a foul. But suppose the ball leaps up the cushion and onto the side, runs along for a while and drops back onto the playing surface? It may even fall into a pocket. In fact, this is a perfectly fair shot, though potting via the rail is not recommended, and if the ball does end up in a pocket you get the points and carry on just as if you had potted it normally.

Equally, you give points away if it is the cue-ball or any ball not 'on' that climbs the rail and drops into a pocket. In other words, if the ball comes back off the rail, you treat it as if it had never gone off. It is where it comes to rest that counts.

However, if the ball goes off and stays on the rail without falling to the ground or returning to the table proper, that is a foul. You clearly cannot continue to play shots with a ball in that position — it would be ridiculous if the ball 'on' could be struck only by making the cue-ball climb up or down the cushion. The rules say that the balls must, at the conclusion of a stroke, be 'on the bed of the table' or in a pocket.

If the cue-ball is forced off the table, it returns to the 'D' and is played from hand. A colour would be re-spotted, and a red put in a pocket.

The jump shot

This stroke, in which the cue-ball is made to leap over an
intervening ball to hit the ball 'on', is no longer permitted.
In any case it was often barred for practical reasons by the
owners of halls, because to play the shot it was necessary to
lay the cue almost flat on the table to get far enough
underneath the ball to make it jump. This often resulted in
ripped cloths and lost tempers. It is now a foul, even if the
cue-ball strikes the object-ball and lands on the far side.
That is still considered to be a jump. It is, however, a fair
shot if the cue-ball 'first strikes the object-ball and then
jumps over another ball'. There is no rule that says the
cue-ball must never leave the surface of the table.

The push shot

The push shot occurs when the cue-tip is judged to be in contact with the cue-ball for longer than is necessary for the striking of the ball. To put it another way, once the cue-ball has started moving, the cue-tip must not be touching it. It is also a foul if the cue-tip is still on the cue-ball when the cue-ball touches the object-ball. This is unavoidable, of course, when cue-ball and object-ball are actually touching at the beginning of a stroke, which is why you have to play away from a touching ball, even if it is 'on'.

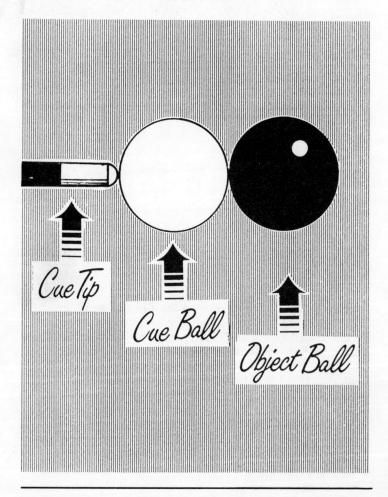

Cue Tip

Cue Ball

Object Ball

It is very difficult when cue-ball and object-ball are almost touching to play the object-ball without 'pushing', so the rules allow you to play a stroke to hit 'the finest possible edge' of the object-ball without penalty.

This is another case where a really competent referee is needed. Judging whether your opponent has pushed, or whether you yourself have done so, requires a degree of detachment and lack of self-interest that might be difficult to achieve at a vital stage of an important frame. Put simply, there might be an almighty row about it.

It is also a foul, by the way, if you strike the cue-ball twice in rapid succession, which you could do by following through too far and too fast.

Will it go?

If you are in a situation where you might or might not be able to squeeze a ball through a gap which might or might not be wide enough, it is very tempting to take a 'dead' ball (that is, one which has already been potted) and put it in the gap to see. Or you might like to put it on the black spot to see if the black you're confident you're going to sink will go back there or will have to go on the pink, which might be less convenient.

This is frowned on, however. You just can't. And it's also a foul if you take a ball off the table, even a spotted one that you know you could put back accurately, if all the balls are still up. You can't even take the cue-ball though perhaps you might like to try it and see what happens . . .

Mind your paunch

You are allowed to touch the cue-ball only with the tip of the cue, and the object balls only with the cue-ball or with other object balls, except of course when you are replacing balls on the table. You are not even allowed, strictly speaking, to pick a ball up to clean it. Only the referee can do that.

This rule means that if you nudge any ball with the side of the cue when getting into position to play a stroke, or with the rest, or if any ball runs into the cue or the rest because you haven't picked them up quickly enough after using them, that is a foul and you have to pay the price. The ball does not have to be moved — a mere touch is enough, and the referee will be watching you.

You can also give away points by touching any ball with your tie, shirt-front, sleeves, cuffs, elbows, paunch, backside, knees and, in extreme cases, feet if you're climbing on the table to get at an awkward one. I have even heard of an elderly player who scrambled up the North Face of the table to play a shot, got stuck fast on the summit as he played it and was hit painfully on the inside of the knee by the cue-ball as it came back off the cushion. The poor chap couldn't get out of the way, but the rules had no compassion for his bad back or his grey hairs. Neither did his opponent, who pointed out to him that his offence came under the heading of 'touching a ball other than with the tip of the cue', looked up the penalty and scored the points, before

calling for help to lift him back off the table. It's a hard world.

The only time you can use anything other than the tip of the cue to move the cue-ball is when positioning the white inside the 'D' when playing from hand. The ball is not then considered to be in play, and so you are not playing a stroke. In that situation you can even use the tip of the cue without the contact counting as a stroke.

The rules also generously allow that a player should not be penalised if the head of the rest falls off and touches a ball. This is covered by the section in the rules called 'Ball moved by other than striker' which says that if a ball is moved or disturbed in any way for which the striker is not responsible, it is re-positioned by the referee. If he happens to disturb the balls, for instance in putting them back on the table or in picking one up to clean it and touching its neighbour, that is not the players' fault. The rule also covers the rather mysterious possibility of 'another agency' causing the striker to touch a ball. That is not the players' fault either.

Feet on the floor

When you've climbed on to the table to play that awkward shot, you must make sure that at least one foot is touching the floor as you play it. You don't have to have your foot flat on the floor with the heel touching; but it is a foul to play a stroke without at least the toe of one shoe on the ground. You are not allowed to lie across the table with your legs in the air, and the referee will be watching to make sure you don't. Snooker is a dignified game. Remember that you are in a snooker hall and not in a bordello in Marseilles.

Record Breaks

The information in this section may not have much relevance to most of us in our daily plod round the old green baize, but maximum breaks are a fascinating subject.

What actually is the maximum break? Well, the obvious answer is 147, made up of fifteen reds, fifteen blacks and all the colours, but it is in fact possible to get as many as 155 in a single visit to the table. This would happen if your opponent fouled with all the reds still on the table and left you a free ball. You would then have to pot the free ball, scoring one, get on the black and pot that, and then set about the fifteen reds and blacks, with eight already on the board. No one has ever been known to achieve this, but it could, in theory, be done. Of course, if you got 155, your aggregate score would actually be at least four points higher because you would get the points for the foul that gave you the free ball. In fact, your opponent could commit any number of fouls, by messing up the break shot repeatedly for instance, before giving you that free ball. So any score is mathematically possible. However, you and I, who don't score even a run-of-the-mill 147 all that often, need not ponder this prospect too long.

Incidentally, for a 147 to be officially recognised, there are three conditions that must be satisfied. The pockets should be of the correct 'cut', a qualified referee should be in charge of the game, and the break must be made in a match to which the public is admitted, presumably so that there are plenty of witnesses.

Stalemate

A stalemate occurs when the situation of the frame has remained unaltered for some time and looks like staying that way, because tactical considerations demand safety play, and the only safe shot either player can make, or is prepared to make, leaves the balls in much the same position as before. This may happen very early in a frame where neither player is prepared to risk smashing up the pack. One will run the cue-ball carefully up to the reds and leave it there, touching or almost touching the nearest red, giving the other the chance to play it away again and leave it on the cushion, from where the first player can simply roll it back onto the pack again. And so the long night wears on and people start to think about doing jigsaw puzzles picture-side down, this being more interesting.

Stalemate probably does not happen often in the ordinary

club social game where someone can usually be relied on to miscalculate the pace or to lose patience and announce, in that bluff way snooker players have, 'Stuff this for a box of soldiers, I'll have a bash and see what happens'. Paying for the table by the minute is another powerful incentive to get a move on.

But if it does look as if the players have the skill and patience to go on rolling up and tapping away for the next fortnight, the referee can warn them that if the deadlock is not broken 'in a short period of time', the frame will be abandoned and will not count in the match. If neither player is then prepared to do anything about it, the referee can step in and re-start the frame. The players continue in the same order — that is, without tossing again to see who breaks.

Leaving the Room

The rules actually make provision for you to leave the room in the course of a frame. This enlightened and humane piece of legislation takes account of the average player's need to pop out and make the odd phone call, put another ten pence in the parking meter and get in his round of drinks during play, and also of the pressures that a tense situation, long hours of concentration and mental strain and two pints a frame can put on the constitution of a sensitive performer.

Your opponent does not have to wait till you come back before he can play his stroke, because you may, in your absence, leave a friend in charge to keep an eye on what the rules call your 'interests'. This could be useful if you suspect

that your opponent is unscrupulous enough to have another go if he doesn't like the result of his first shot, but snooker players are a fine upstanding class of person, renowned for high moral character, and are unlikely to stoop to such dastardly actions. The substitute is more likely to be needed to claim a foul if one is committed — something might happen in the course of a stroke that the striker genuinely does not notice, such as brushing a ball with a shirt-sleeve. Of course, if you had a referee, you'd expect him to notice that. The rule does not say whether the substitute has the power to ask the striker to play again after a foul, or whether this decision has to await the return of the absentee himself. The substitute does not have the right to play a stroke.

Sitting Out

On leaving the table, at which point a stroke is formally ended, most professionals have a long last look at the golden opportunity or terrible mess they have left for their opponent, shake their heads and retire to a distant chair and a nice glass of mineral water. This is in accordance with the rule which says that the non-striker 'should sit or stand at a fair distance from the table' and should not stand or move in the opponent's line of sight.

In a friendly social game, especially a four-hander, the players often lounge around the table, explaining where the ball should have gone or pretending that the situation facing the next player is exactly what they were after. It is the time for the snooker player's sparkling wit ('That was supposed to stop' — 'It will, soon'). The comedy routines and tactical exchanges are not, of course, intended to put the striker off his stroke, which would come under the heading of 'unfair conduct', but they don't do much for his concentration. Standing over the pocket the striker is aiming to pot into and muttering, 'That won't go past that pink, not in a million years, my son' or 'You're in here, Mike, he'll never pot it' doesn't help either.

Unfair Conduct

Getting in the striker's line of sight and doing your Ted Lowe impression, or tapping with your cue on the floor while he's addressing the ball, and all that sort of thing, comes under the heading of unfair conduct, which covers anything 'which in the opinion of the referee is wilfully or persistently unfair'. Notice that the offence must be deliberate and repeated — one isolated incident, perhaps not intentional, is not enough to lose you the frame on a disqualification. Refusing to continue a frame, perhaps in disagreement with a decision, can get you disqualified, but going out for urgent personal reasons, as described above, does not count as refusing to continue. In fact, many players would regard refusing to get your round in as a much more serious offence.

Time-wasting — that is, 'taking an abnormal amount of time over a stroke' — is of course unfair, and can provoke the referee into warning the offender that he risks disqualification.

If disqualified, the player loses the game. He also forfeits all points scored and, in the words of the rule 'the non-offender shall receive the value of the balls still on the table (each red counting eight points)'. This is important in competitions where aggregate scores can decide who goes through to the next round.

A disqualified player guilty of some really serious offence against fair play could face disqualification from tournaments held under the auspices of the governing body and of bodies affiliated to it. It is pleasant to be able to say, however, that the game has a fine reputation for sportsmanship, and conduct likely to lead to disqualification is extremely rare. Let's keep it that way.

Fouls

A foul is 'any act in contravention' of the rules. When one
occurs, the referee announces 'Foul' and waits till all the
balls have stopped moving, in case something worse
happens. He then pronounces sentence. The break
automatically stops, but all points scored before the foul
stroke was played, count. This means that the break up to
that point is safe, but the striker does not score any points
for a stroke in which a foul is committed. So, if you pot a red
legally and then put the cue-ball in, you do not get a point
for the red. You just concede the penalty points. The next
stroke is played from where the cue-ball comes to rest,
unless of course it has gone in-off or right off the table. If it
has, it is returned to the 'D' and played 'from hand'. It can
also be put back in the 'D' if it is angled as the result of a
foul.

You would normally play the next shot yourself after your opponent's break ends, but if it ends in a foul, you can ask him to play again from where he has left the cue-ball. You do not have to be snookered to be able to put your opponent 'in' again — you can ask him to play from any position he has left you which you don't happen to fancy, one for example in which there is no chance of a pot and all you have is a tricky safety shot. Once you have asked, you are not allowed to change your mind and play it yourself. If your opponent spots an opening you missed and clears up, that's too bad. If you are snookered as the result of a foul, you have the right to a free ball.

If the foul is not noticed by the referee or claimed by the other player before the next shot is played, it is said to have been condoned, which means that you cannot claim ten minutes later when you're a long way behind that you saw your opponent nudge a ball with his sleeve, and that will be four . . . Your opponent would be quite right to say that you should have mentioned it earlier. A partial exception to this is the case of players playing on with the balls wrongly spotted, as described in 'Re-spotting' on pages 20–3.

If two fouls are committed in the same stroke, the highest always counts. So if reds are 'on' and you miss them all, hit pink and black and pot them both, that's seven away. We say 'seven away', but the seven go on to the non-offender's score rather than being subtracted from the offender's. The scoreboard has no space for minuses, which is just as well for some of us.

Penalties

There are twenty different ways of committing a foul, each carrying a penalty of greater or lesser severity. The absolute minimum is four, even though the reds, the yellow and the green are worth only one, two and three respectively.

The commonest acts of folly are these:

1. 'Causing the cue-ball to enter a pocket' — that is, going in directly or in-off another ball. The penalty varies for this. If you go in directly, that is without hitting any other ball, the penalty is the value of the ball 'on'. So, if you were on a red, the penalty would be four, but if you were on blue it would be five, and so on. The same applies if you go in-off after first striking the ball 'on' — the value of the ball 'on' decides the penalty. You may, however, be on a red, miss it, hit the black and go in-off that. Here, in fact, the penalty is not for going in-off but for missing the ball 'on' and hitting something else (see 3 below). The penalty for that is the value of the ball 'on' or of the ball hit, whichever is the greater. In this case you hit the black, so it's seven.

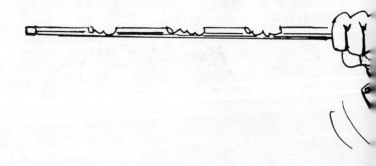

You may even be on a red, miss it, hit the brown and then the pink and go in-off. What do you make of that series of disasters? Well, the penalty is four, not six. Again, the penalty is for first striking a ball not 'on', not for going in-off it. The brown was the first ball you hit, so it's four. Similarly, if you hit the pink first after missing the red and the cue-ball finally went in-off the black, the penalty would be six, not seven, because you hit the pink first.

Don't forget that if you are playing away from a touching ball, you are not allowed to pocket the cue-ball. If you do, you give away the value of the ball 'on' or of the first ball struck on the way, whichever is the higher.

2. If the cue-ball misses all the balls, the penalty is the value of the ball 'on', whether the cue-ball stays up or goes down as in 1 above.

3. You could, of course, not only miss the ball you were aiming at, but strike one not 'on' as well. It is a foul (unless you are playing away from a touching ball which is 'on'), and the penalty is the value of the ball 'on' or of the ball first struck. If you are playing for blue and hit the pink and then the black, the penalty is six. On the other hand, if you play for the pink, miss it and hit blue, the penalty is still six, as the pink here is the ball 'on'. It does not matter in either case that you went on to hit the black. It would, however, make things worse if you potted it, as we shall see now.

4. It is a foul to pot a ball which is not 'on', even if you are playing away from a touching ball. The penalty is the usual one — the value of the ball 'on' or of the ball potted, whichever is the greater. So, if you play the blue and end up potting the yellow, the penalty is five. If you play the yellow, hit it and then pot the blue, the penalty is again five.

There is also the nightmare possibility of hitting the ball 'on', then hitting two other balls which are not 'on' and potting them both. If you did this, the penalty would be the value of the higher of the two illegally potted, or of the ball 'on' if that was higher than either, but you might feel in this circumstance that the only decent thing to do would be to sharpen your cue, go outside and fall on it.

Then there are several less common misdemeanours . . .

5. Playing before all the balls have stopped moving from the previous shot, whether your own or your opponent's, will cost you the value of the ball 'on'. However, it may be more if you commit another foul in the same shot. Remember, the rules say that if more than one foul is committed in the same stroke, the highest penalty is exacted. Playing at a red before the balls have stopped would automatically cost you four, but if you potted the black in the same shot, it would go up to seven.

6. If you play with the balls not placed on their proper spots or not re-spotted at all, the penalty is the value of the ball 'on' or of the ball in question, whichever is higher. So, if you played at a red (the ball 'on') with the black wrongly spotted or still in a pocket, the penalty would be seven. To avoid the risk of losing points in this situation, it is handy to know the rule about where to spot colours when their own spots are occupied. Remember that one? If not, go back to pages 20–3 and miss two turns.

As in 5, you could forfeit more points if you played with a ball incorrectly spotted and then did something more serious in the same stroke.

This seems a good moment to remind you that it is your responsibility, not the referee's, to see that the balls are in the right place.

7. If you touch a ball other than with the tip of the cue — and, of course, the cue-ball is the only ball you are ever allowed to touch with any part of the cue — the penalty is the value of the ball 'on' or of the ball touched. Therefore, if you are lining up on a red and touch the pink with your hand, you give away six, the pink being the higher of the two.

8. For forcing a ball off the table, you forfeit the value of that ball, or of the ball 'on'. If the cue-ball and the ball 'on' are both forced off, then the penalty is the value of the ball 'on', which must be at least four, four being the minimum penalty. If the cue-ball and more than one other ball are forced off, then the penalty is either the value of the ball 'on' or the value of the higher of the two object-balls forced off, assuming that that is higher than the value of the ball 'on'. So, if you are on the blue, hit it and somehow contrive to force white, pink and black off the table, the penalty is seven; but if you play blue and force off white and two reds, or green and brown, the penalty is five. This is hardly likely, of course, but stranger things have happened.

9. If you hit two balls at once, the penalty is either the value of the ball 'on' or the value of the higher of the two balls hit. If you're trying to hit a red, and hit it and the blue at the same time, the penalty is five. If you're having one of those days when you wish you'd never got up and you miss the red you're 'on' and hit green and pink simultaneously, that costs you six.

You will remember that you are allowed to hit two reds at the same time, or a nominated ball and the ball 'on', without penalty.

10. Hitting the cue-ball more than once in the course of a stroke will cost you the value of the ball 'on'. But this is another example of the rule that says that if any further foul is committed in the course of the stroke, the highest value penalty will count.

11. Playing a push stroke means that you forfeit the value of the ball 'on' or of the ball concerned, the higher, as always, being the one that counts; and you could, again, cause further damage and incur a higher penalty later in the same stroke. Bear in mind that it is a push stroke if you don't play away from a touching ball, even if it is 'on'.

12. For playing a jump shot, the penalty is the value of the ball 'on', with the same proviso about subsequent and more expensive fouls.

13. You are not allowed to leave your opponent snookered behind the ball you nominated when you were awarded a free ball, unless only the pink and black are left on the table. If you do, you are penalised the value of the ball 'on'.

14. Having both legs in the air when you play a shot is not only inelegant, it's illegal. You will pay for this offence against dignity by forfeiting the value of the ball 'on', unless, again, you commit another and more expensive foul.

15. If you play out of turn, more likely of course in a four-hander than in an individual match, you give away the value of the ball 'on', unless, of course, you commit another more serious foul in the same shot. The referee will not give 'any indication' that you are about to break the rules by doing this, or indeed by doing anything else, but will jump on you with both feet if you do.

16. In the same way, if you are 'in hand' but play with the ball actually outside the 'D', you lose the value of the ball 'on', except as usual in the event of your going on to do something worse. If you are not sure whether you are playing correctly, with the ball inside the 'D' or on the lines, you can ask the referee. He is allowed to tell you that.

17. You may find yourself in the situation where you have just potted a red and are thinking about which colour to go for. You could, while still making up your mind, commit a foul. You might, for instance, touch a ball with your sleeve while leaning over to see if one will go. If you do, you cannot apply the usual 'value of the ball "on" or of the ball touched' formula, because, as you have not nominated, there is no ball 'on'. The rules take the worst possible view of this unhappy position and exact seven.

18. Using a 'dead' ball to see if there is room for a shot, or for any other reason, will cost you seven, regardless of which ball you use to commit this outrage.

19. Having a rush of blood to the head and playing at two successive reds instead of a red and a colour is, on the face of it, not all that likely, but it could happen, and the penalty for doing it is seven.

20. It is also rather unlikely that anyone would so forget himself as to use any ball but the white as the cue-ball, but the rules do make provision for this act of half-wittedness, just in case. The half-wit in question forfeits seven, regardless of which ball he mistakes for the white. Colour-blind players have no excuse. They can ask the referee where the cue-ball is and that kind-hearted official will tell them.

It seems safe to assume that you are allowed to do anything the rules do not actually forbid. Simple game, eh? Nothing to it.

End of the Game

A frame is over when one player concedes that the situation is hopeless, or when the last black is potted or fouled, or, very rarely, when a player is disqualified for unfair play.

The frame automatically ends if the pink is finally potted and the difference in scores is more than seven. You cannot play on hoping that your opponent will foul and let you in again. If the pink is still up, however, the player who is behind can go on trying to get the snookers that will bring him within seven points, however great the deficit. Most players will already have conceded if they need more than one snooker, though.

If the result of the frame depends on who pots the black (a black-ball game) the frame continues until the black is potted or fouled, unless the seven points scored in this way mean the scores become level. If this happens, the black is re-spotted and the cue-ball placed in the 'D'. The players then toss (the rules say 'draw lots') to see who re-starts, regardless of who potted or fouled the black, and of the order of play throughout the frame. The winner of the toss can put his opponent in, but usually takes the shot himself. The frame ends the next time the black is either potted or fouled, even though a foul that left the black still on the table would seem to give the player who fouled the chance to pot the black if his opponent fails to, and so to draw level again.

As a note to this section, the rules say that in matches where aggregate scores count the black is re-spotted in this way only when the scores are equal as a result of the last frame.

Playing as a Team

You can play snooker as a team or as individuals. Most doubles matches are social occasions, though of course there are serious doubles events, and 'four-handers' are as remarkable for the dazzling repartee they inspire as for the deadly potting and canny safety play of those privileged to take part.

It is inevitable that the partners in this feast of skill should want to consult on the finer tactical points and to insult each other from time to time for letting the opposition in. The rules allow players to 'confer', but make it clear that this must not happen 'whilst the striker is at the table'. The non-strikers should avoid doing anything that will put the striker off his stroke. Advice and abuse should be exchanged in whispers and sign language in a distant corner well out of the line of sight.

In a four-handed match, you can change the order of play (who follows whom) only between frames. If you change it during a frame, deliberately or by forgetting whose turn it is, you leave yourself liable to the dreadful penalties prescribed by the rules for playing out of turn.

If there is a foul and the other team exercises its option of putting the offender in again, the player who committed the foul has to play the stroke. He can't pass it on to his partner, however much better he's playing.

If the black has to be re-spotted because the scores are level, the team which is to play the first shot can decide who is going to play it. Whoever has been following that player must play next, so as to maintain the order of play that was followed in the original frame.

The Referee

The referee is a god-like presence who patrols our television screens in a penguin suit and white gloves, calling the score and telling the crowd to pipe down. He also knows the rules. The rules are written on the assumption that there is always a referee in charge, but his solemn duties descend on our shoulders most of the time, as we generally have to referee our games as well as play in them.

The referee is responsible for judging 'fair and unfair play' and for seeing that the game is conducted according to the rules. He must intervene if he sees any rule being infringed, but he does not warn a player that he is about to infringe one. It is the players' responsibility to know the rules as well.

The referee calls 'foul' as soon as one is committed, and awards the penalty points. He announces 'touching ball', 'angled ball' and 'free ball' without being asked, will require a player to nominate if he is in any doubt about which ball the player is trying to hit first, and will answer if asked whether a ball is placed properly within the limits of the 'D'.

He will not, however, 'answer any question not authorised in the rules' and will not 'give any advice or opinion on points affecting play'. So, it's no good going to him with your little problems.

If the referee does not notice a foul and it is not claimed by the opposition before the next stroke is made, it is condoned, as explained earlier. If anything escapes the referee's merciless scrutiny, and is claimed, he is allowed to 'take the evidence' of onlookers in a good position to see to help him to make his decision.

The referee will also clean the balls if requested to do so — the players themselves are not allowed to do this — and he also has the power to have a set of balls changed if he thinks they are too worn or of uneven weight.

If a player is colour-blind, the referee will point out the different colours to him. He will also warn the players if a state of stalemate is approaching (see pages 44–5), and may warn a player of the need to play his shots more quickly, as discussed in 'Slow play'. He may in extreme cases disqualify a player for 'wilful and persistent unfair conduct'.

That's the referee's job. To help him, he may have the services of the marker . . .

The Marker

The marker is not seen much, but he merits a small section to himself in the rules. His main duty is to keep the score on the 'marking board', and he is also instructed to help the referee in the conduct of matches.

The rules lay one more duty on the officials. In the event of a light shade interfering with a player's ability to get into position to play a shot, the referee or marker may, if asked, move the offending shade and hold it out of the way so that the player can play unobstructed. That's the caring society for you.

Conclusion

Snooker, then, is a bit more complicated than it looks as you watch those immaculate professionals running up their century breaks and shaking hands with the sponsor. The pint you win may not put you in their league as a money-earner, but it would be a shame to lose it because you awarded four against yourself when the head of the rest fell off and fouled the yellow.

Snooker rules – OK?

Index